Divorce

Anne Charlish

RSVP

RAINTREE
STECK-VAUGHN
P U B L I S H E R S
A Steck-Vaughn Company

Austin, Texas

Published by Raintree Steck-Vaughn Publishers, an imprint of Steck-Vaughn Company

Library of Congress Cataloging-in-Publication Data
Charlish, Anne.
Divorce / Anne Charlish.
      p.   cm.—(Talking points)
      Includes bibliographical references and index.
      Summary: Discusses divorce in today's world and in the past, legal and financial issues related to it, and the effects of divorce upon children and society. Includes case studies.
      ISBN 0-8172-5310-6
      1. Divorce—Juvenile literature.
      2. Children of divorced parents—Juvenile literature.
      [1. Divorce.]
      I. Title. II. Series.
HQ814.C46 1999
306.89—dc21   98-6038

Printed in Italy. Bound in the United States.
1 2 3 4 5 6 7 8 9 0 03 02 01 00 99

Acknowledgments
The author would like to thank the following organizations for their valuable assistance: ChildLine, Families Need Fathers, London Marriage Guidance Council, Muslim Information Center, National Family Mediation, National Stepfamily Association, One Plus One, Relate, Reunite. The author would also like to thank the following individuals for their kind support: Monica Cockett, Dr. John Tripp, Professor Richard A. Warshak, Professor Henry Biller, Altan Ural, Tamara, Süreyya, Ton, Helena, Diana, and Susannah.

Picture acknowledgments
Bubbles Photo Library 5 (Jennie Woodcock), 7 (Peter Sylent), 8 (Peter Sylent), 10 (Jennie Woodcock), 26 (Peter Sylent), 32 (Frans Rombout), 39 (Ian West), 47 (Peter Sylent), 48 (Peter Sylent), 58 (Jennie Woodcock); Mary Evans Picture Library 13, 15, 17, 18, 19; Eye Ubiquitous 44 (J Gibb); Format Photographers 28 (Paula Solloway), 34 (Brenda Prince), 35 (Judy Harrison), 37 (Ulrike Preuss), 38 (Jacky Chapman); Getty Images 4 (Jon Riley), 6 (Jon Riley), 11, 12 (Steven Peters), 20 (Keren Su), 21 (Dan Bosler), 24 (David Young Wolff), 30 (Stewart Cohen), 33 (Peter Correz), 36 (Mark Douet), 41 (Kate Connell), 42 (Zigy Kaluzny), 49 (Penny Tweedie), 51 (Tony Latham), 53 (Ian O'Leary), 54 (Bruce Ayres); Sally and Richard Greenhill 23, 43; Angela Hampton Family Life Pictures 9, 31, 59; Hulton Getty Picture Collection 14; Retna Pictures Limited 40 (Grace Huang); Wayland Picture Library 50 (Tizzie Knowles), 56.

Contents

What is divorce?

Talking point

"Everybody wants to keep wraps on the whole thing... the hidden pain is really unbearable. Children don't want to ask about the divorce; parents don't want to talk about it, and that's one very powerful reason for the conspiracy of silence about the painful effects of divorce."

Dr. Sebastian Kraemer, consultant, child and adolescent psychiatrist

Do you agree that there is a "conspiracy of silence" about the effects of divorce?

Divorce is the legal term for the end of a marriage between two people. Marriage exists in most societies around the world, and where there is marriage there is generally divorce. If a husband and wife split up without obtaining a divorce, they are still married to each other, even though they live apart. (If they were not married in the first place, we would say that they were "breaking up" or "splitting up.") Before the divorce is completed, or finalized, the husband and wife usually choose to live apart. This period is known as separation. Once the divorce is legally finalized, the partners are free to marry someone else.

The majority of those who marry tend to regard it as a lifetime commitment. Few people marry with the intention of getting divorced. However, some couples reach a point when they feel that they can

no longer continue in their marriage. During separation and divorce the marriage partners usually experience a variety of emotions, including anger, guilt, fear, anxiety—and relief, if the marriage has been troubled for some time. In their marriage, the couple had probably hoped for a stable and happy relationship for the rest of their lives and a secure and happy framework in which to bring up their children. Divorce brings with it, inevitably, a dashing of these hopes, combined with psychological distress, money worries, and concern for the feelings of the children of the marriage.

During the process of divorce, arrangements are made to divide the couple's finances. Arrangements are also made for the care of any children resulting from the marriage. Separation and divorce are often acutely painful for children. When two people divorce, one parent normally leaves the family home to live somewhere else. The children may continue to see this parent from time to time, but they will no longer enjoy family life in the way that they used to.

A wedding usually involves the bride and groom taking vows of loyalty and fidelity to each other. Their marriage vows are meant to last for the rest of their lives, but not all marriages survive.

The ideal for the child is a family with two loving parents who are happy with each other. Many children are so threatened by the idea of their parents' divorce that they would prefer that they stay together no matter how things are at home.

"My Mom and Dad were always shouting at each other—or else they didn't talk at all. My Mom was often crying and telling us to go to our rooms. Now Dad doesn't live here and Mom is better. She spends more time with us and she doesn't shout at us. But I wish Dad still lived with us."

Nine-year-old boy

Grounds for divorce

In many countries in the West, there has been one ground for divorce: the irretrievable breakdown of marriage. According to the law, one partner has to prove that the marriage has broken down by establishing one of five facts. These include adultery (meaning that one—or both—of the partners has had a sexual relationship with someone outside the marriage), unreasonable behavior, desertion (of at least two years' duration), separation (meaning that the partners have lived apart for at least two years, and that they both consent to a divorce) and separation of at least five years' duration (whether or not the partners agree to the divorce). Divorces on the "fault" grounds of adultery or unreasonable behavior can be processed in as few as three months.

However, the process of making one person "the one at fault" can lead to couples, whose marriages might have been saved, splitting up too quickly. Apportioning blame can cause anger and resentment between the marriage partners and distress for any children that might be involved. In the United States, the irretrievable breakdown of marriage is the one common ground for divorce. Each of the 50 states has passed its own laws to determine when a marriage is irretrievably broken. In New Jersey, one partner has to prove that the marriage is broken down by establishing one of eight facts. These facts include adultery, extreme cruelty, desertion, or separation.

Many couples have regular disagreements over money, but only in some cases does this contribute to the breakdown of the marriage.

Is it the same for everyone?

All families are different. Many married couples argue and fight, but nevertheless continue to stay together. Others, while appearing to be fairly happy and settled, may break up with little warning. In the same way, the experience of divorce differs from family to family and from individual to individual. Most adults and children are devastated by the end of a marriage, experiencing it as a profound loss or bereavement. Others tend to see the failure of their marriage as inevitable and, although marked by the experience, they make a concerted effort to put it behind them and embrace a new way of life.

> "There were three of us in this marriage... so it was a bit crowded."
>
> Diana, Princess of Wales, talking about her marriage to Prince Charles. Diana argued that her husband's affair with another woman had been instrumental in the breakup of their marriage.

The experience of divorce varies not only from person to person but also from culture to culture. The way that people view divorce in the West (which includes Europe, North America, and Australia) differs from how people view divorce in Japan or in the Arab world. Throughout history, attitudes to divorce have varied greatly too. In the past, divorce was commonly regarded as unthinkable. Regardless of whether they were happy or not, couples were expected to live out their marriages until death parted them. Today, high divorce rates in the West show that attitudes have changed.

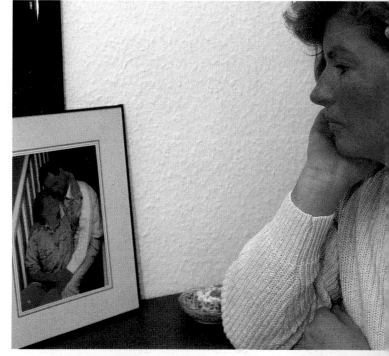

It can take many years to accept that one's marriage has ended in divorce. Some people continue to regret their divorce for the rest of their lives.

A relationship or marriage in which violence is perceived as a normal part of everyday life can be very damaging to children. Alcohol abuse is often linked with instances of domestic violence.

Who gets divorced?

It is difficult to generalize about the types of people most likely to divorce, but there are several categories of persons that seem to run a statistical risk of ending up in a failed marriage. For example, the offspring of divorced parents run a higher risk of divorcing than the offspring of intact families. Those who marry while still in their teens are also more likely to divorce than couples who marry in their twenties. A young couple may rush into marriage to escape their parents or because the girl is pregnant, but their romantic ideals of what marriage should be like soon begin to crumble when they find themselves living on a low income in poor housing. These problems, coupled with their extreme youth, which may render them unable to judge what each

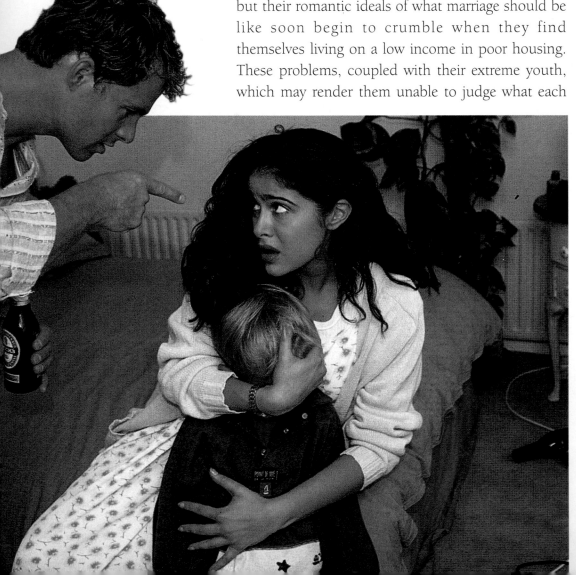

When a marriage breaks down

The legal grounds chosen for divorce tend to conceal a wide range of symptoms that suggest that a marriage is in danger. These symptoms may include prolonged and angry arguments about money, housework, children, and sex; violence by one partner against another; life changes (such as the birth of a first child, a new job for one partner, a move to a new area in which one or both of the partners may be unhappy, the death of a close family member, serious illness in the family, job loss, or retirement); jealousy (whether or not there is reason for suspicion); falling in love with someone else; falling out of love with each other and wanting different things from life; alcoholism or drug abuse, which makes one partner difficult or impossible to live with.

of them needs and wants from the marriage, make them more likely to divorce.

Poverty and financial difficulties often have a part to play in the breakdown of a marriage, particularly today when there is less support from parents and the wider family than there used to be in the past. Couples in which one partner suddenly loses a job, goes bankrupt, or has a criminal conviction run an increased risk of experiencing divorce.

Teenage pregnancy can lead to a quick, early marriage, which may prove frail. Such relationships run an increased risk of ending in divorce with both partners recognizing that they married too young.

A marriage made later in life may be troubled if the couple cannot adapt to each other's needs.

Couples who are on their second marriages are also more likely to divorce. Older people who decide to marry may already be set in their ways and may find it difficult to adapt to living with someone else. Those who re-marry may have done so in haste to escape an unhappy first marriage; but they may find that problems from their first marriage haunt their second. And, if both partners have children, they may have difficulties trying to bring both families together in harmony.

> "I see my Dad once a week. Sometimes he takes me to the movies, sometimes we go to the park. Then he takes me for a burger and then he takes me home to Mom. I can't remember when he lived with us at home. My mom divorced him a long time ago."
>
> Thirteen-year-old girl

Cause for regret?

In law, divorce describes one single event—the end of a marriage. But in reality it represents the slow breakdown of a relationship that probably started out full of love and hope. No wonder, then, that divorce is a cause of sadness and regret: 51 percent of men and 29 percent of women who have divorced wish that their marriages had not been dissolved. Most children of divorced parents wish that the couple had stayed together; and, even after the divorce, most children continue to hope that their parents will get back together again. The following words of a teenage girl describe the loneliness and isolation that children of divorced parents can feel: "I look around me and most of my friends have got parents together and they didn't have problems like I did when I was younger. So, in some ways, that's why it hurts so much."

A marriage starts out full of hope and love and regard for each other; but figures show that not all marriages can be sustained through the bad times.

Case study

Martin, a forty-five-year-old New York businessman, talks about the events leading to his divorce.

"We met when we were both in our early twenties, having just finished college overseas. We were immediately fascinated by one another. It was as if we had found our missing sections— we fitted together beautifully. We became really close. We were, I think, each other's best friends. She never bored me. It was a very passionate, very entwined relationship. She agreed to come and live with me back in the States. From there, everything just followed on naturally. We got married, traveled around for a bit, and then we settled down. She landed a brilliant job —a real coup. Everything looked great.

The pressures of work and family placed too great a strain on Martin's marriage.

"We were both working extremely hard and she was fascinated by her job. She was just as ambitious as I. When we had our first child, she coped with the conflicting demands of home and office very well. But once our second child came along, the strains really started to show. She was constantly exhausted and used to fall asleep in front of the television every night by nine o'clock. Each morning was a mad rush to get the youngest to day care and the older child to school. She didn't have time to look after herself properly or take care of her appearance. I felt that she wasn't interested in me sexually anymore. All she wanted to do was sleep. When she was awake, she would be snappish with me and the children. It was simply all too much. I wanted some joy, some fun in my life. I met someone else, and in the end we agreed to divorce. It does seem a terrible waste, though."

Divorce in the past

Talking point

The father is entitled to custody of his own children during their infancy, not only as guardian by nurture, but by nature... If he can in any way gain them, he is at liberty to do so, provided no breach of the peace be made in such an attempt."

From a British lord chancellor's speech in 1732

his speech describes the nrivaled powers that ighteenth-century fathers ossessed in regard to ustody of their children. In hat way do you think ttitudes have changed?

In the West, the institutions of marriage and divorce are based on ancient Hebrew and Roman traditions. In biblical times, according to Jewish law, a wife did not have the right to divorce her husband but she could marry again if her husband divorced her. In the Roman Empire, marriage was not a legal requirement. Men and women simply lived together in a permanent household. Roman law required only that they be above the age of puberty and had the consent of their families. Either partner could end the marriage by written application to the authorities.

> "When a man takes a wife and marries her, if then she finds no favor in his eyes because he has found some indecency in her...he writes her a bill of divorce and puts it in her hand and sends her out of his house and she departs out of his house...."
>
> Deuteronomy 24:1

Divorce in the West is based on Hebrew and Roman traditions. This picture shows a Jewish couple obtaining a divorce in biblical times, more than 2,000 years ago.

The early Christian emperors of Rome started to bring marriage and divorce under the authority of the law. From the Middle Ages onward, the marriage of two people was held to be a sacred and unbreakable contract, in accordance with the beliefs of the Catholic Church. In Germany in the sixteenth century, Martin Luther and other Protestants broke away from the Roman Catholic faith and set up a separate church. The Protestants permitted divorce in specific circumstances, such as cruelty, adultery, and desertion.

Henry VIII of England divorced his first wife, Catherine of Aragon (pictured above, kneeling), so he could marry again. His divorce prompted a split between the English monarch and the Roman Catholic Church.

In England divorce became legal when Henry VIII broke away from the Roman Catholic Church in order to divorce his first wife, Catherine of Aragon, in 1534. But every divorce that took place required a separate act of Parliament, which meant that divorce was extremely expensive and only available to the rich and well-connected.

In previous centuries, men were able to subdue noisy or quarrelsome wives with a brank, or scold's bridle. This device had an iron curb for the tongue, which was held in place by a frame around the head.

The role of women

For many centuries, married women in the Christian West were regarded by their husbands as property. Though living in a "free society," wives were treated like slaves. Until the nineteenth century, a married woman was completely under the control of her husband: her body, her property, her earnings, and her children were all the husband's to do with as he wished. From about 1650 on, married couples could apply for "articles of separation," which would allow them to live separately. Alternatively, either husband or wife could abandon the marriage and go and live somewhere else. However, while many men possessed the means to do this, most women did not. Their possessions were the property of their husbands, whose duty it was to provide food and shelter.

The wife sale

A husband's duty was to provide for his wife, whether or not the marriage was to his liking. But husbands were able to get around this obligation by selling their wives at market—in the same way that they could legally sell any of their possessions. In this way, a husband could pass on his marital obligations to the buyer who then had a duty to provide the woman with food and shelter. She, in turn, became the property of the buyer. Wife sales were known throughout England in the two hundred years between 1650 and 1850. They were usually carried out by poor people. Wealthier people would either establish two households, apply for a judicial separation, or separate informally.

"...he puts a halter about her neck, and thereby leads her to the next market place, and there puts her up to auction to be sold to the best bidder, as though she was a brood-mare or a milch-cow."

An observer of a wife sale, writing in 1777

In England in the seventeenth, eighteenth, and nineteenth centuries, poorer men who could not afford to divorce were able to sell their wives at market. Once their marital obligations had been passed on to a buyer, the men were entitled to marry again.

Divorce in North America

Until the sixteenth century, Christians regarded marriage as a binding contract. But the Protestant Reformation led to the idea that divorce should be a matter for the government rather than for the church. By the nineteenth century, the divorce rate in the United States was higher than that of other countries. Between 1867 and 1907 there were 1,274,341 divorces in the United States and only 431 in Canada. Divorce was 230 times more frequent in the

United States than in Canada, even allowing for the difference in populations. Divorce law in the United States depended on which state you lived in. By the end of the nineteenth century, a divorce was easy to obtain in some states, such as Nevada, and nearly impossible in others. By the 1940s, divorce procedures had become more sensible and reasonable in all states.

This contemporary postcard illustrates the ease with which a couple could obtain a divorce in 1920s Nevada. By contrast, it was difficult, if not impossible, to achieve a divorce in other North American states.

An illegal relationship

In sixteenth- and seventeenth-century England, and in some states of America, it was an offense for married couples not to live with each other. In New England, in 1676 a woman was charged with "leaving the fellowship of her husband." The woman defended herself by saying that she found life with her husband intolerable and that he had been unable to satisfy her sexually. She was fined and the pair were ordered to get back together again.

THE GREAT BOON.

Superior Being (!). "YOU'LL PLEASE TO OBSERVE, MUM, THAT A DIVORCE IS A MUCH EASIER MATTER THAN IT USED TO BE—SO NONE OF YOUR VIOLENCE!"

The cartoon above comments wryly about the state of marriage and divorce law in early twentieth century Great Britain. A bullying husband lectures his cowering wife about the ease with which he can now divorce her.

England's first divorce law was passed in 1857, but public disapproval of divorce counted for much in the social climate of the Victorian age, and wives were still regarded as very much the property of their husbands. Up to the beginning of the twentieth century, the only possible grounds for the dissolution of a marriage in the Western world were adultery or desertion of more than seven years' duration. It was not until the 1920s in the West that women won the right, for the first time, to divorce on the same grounds as men.

Changing attitudes

When considering the historical aspects of divorce in the Western world, several important factors should

"…it must be carefully remembered that the general happiness of the married life is secured by its indissolubility. When people understand that they must live together, except for a very few reasons known to the law, they learn to soften by mutual accommodation that yoke which they know they cannot shake off, and they become good husbands and good wives—from the necessity of remaining husbands and wives—for necessity is a powerful master in teaching the duties of life."

Extract from a debate in the House of Lords, London, 1853

be borne in mind. In previous centuries, life was much shorter than it is today. A typical marriage would last 20 to 30 years at the most, before death intervened. Death rates were higher in all age groups. Many marriages ended after only a few years with the death of one partner, leaving the other free to marry again. Among women, the high incidence of death in childbirth resulted in many single-parent families, stepfamilies, and motherless children. Religion played a huge part in people's lives, and divorce was regarded by many as an affront in the eyes of God.

This French postcard from 1858 jokes about the tribulations of marriage—showing the same woman as proud fiancée, weeping wife, and, finally, joyful divorcée.

Increasing industrialization and the large-scale movement of the population from rural villages to cities has meant that families are more scattered than they used to be. In earlier times, it was common to find several generations of one family in the same village. As people began to travel to towns and cities to find work, the support network of the extended family diminished. There were greater distances between family members, so their opportunities to observe and help resolve marital problems were sharply reduced.

The extended family network of parents, grandparents, uncles, and aunts (below) contributed to the strength of marriage in times past and, indeed, still does In some cultures today. In the West, however, its role has greatly declined. ▼

Women's expectations are higher now than they were in centuries gone by. Their increased economic independence means that they are no longer compelled to stay in unhappy marriages for financial reasons. Widely available and efficient contraception allows them to limit the number of children they have. No longer regarded as the property of their husbands, they can choose to go to work or remain

Today women expect ▶ more from life than their counterparts did a century ago. They have a level of economic freedom that was denied them in the past, and they can sue for divorce on the same grounds as men.

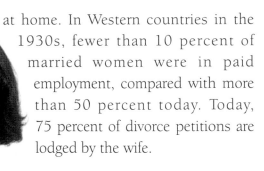

at home. In Western countries in the 1930s, fewer than 10 percent of married women were in paid employment, compared with more than 50 percent today. Today, 75 percent of divorce petitions are lodged by the wife.

Other cultures

Divorce is not just a modern Western phenomenon. Some other cultures have seen high divorce rates in past centuries as well as today. Japan was believed to have had a relatively stable divorce rate for centuries, but it is impossible to obtain figures because marriage practices were governed by local custom and no state licence was (or is) required for marriage. It was not uncommon for the marriage to be recorded some time after the ceremony, so that if the new daughter-in-law proved unsatisfactory, the family could send her back to her original family. In this way, separations were conducted on an informal basis, and no records were kept.

In Japan in the 1880s there were some 300 official divorces out of 1,000 marriages—but the true figure is believed to be much higher. Even this figure is surprisingly high for the time, at nearly 30 percent. Japan's Civil Code of 1898 required marriages to be registered with the state. After that time, divorces went unrecorded unless the marriage had also been recorded. The Japanese divorce rate reached its lowest figure in the early 1960s and then started to rise once again in the mid-1980s.

There is less data on divorce in the Arab world than in the Western world. This can be explained by the fact that divorce in Muslim countries was not traditionally disapproved of in the way that it was in Christian cultures (for 800 years, divorce was not possible in the West). While the Koran, the holy book of Islam, disapproves of divorce, it does not absolutely forbid it. The divorce rates for Arab countries are relatively stable by comparison with those in the West, and some are even in decline.

Divorce rate in Japan from 1885 to present	
Year	Divorce rate per 1,000 population
1885	3.4
1890	2.65
1900	1.45
1910	1.20
1920	1.00
1930	0.80
1940	0.60
1950	1.01
1955	0.84
1960	0.74
1963	0.73
1965	0.79
1970	0.93
1975	1.07
1980	1.22
1986	1.37
1988	1.26
1990	1.28
1995	1.6

"Unlike non-Muslim marriages in the West, where premarital love and intimacy are considered to be almost indispensable, the basic ingredient for a successful Muslim marriage is a shared set of values upon which to build a life together. A firm, shared belief in Islam can often bind couples together in their relationships which can then withstand many of the pressures which force non-Muslim couples apart."

The Muslim Educational Trust, 1997

Arranged marriages

Arranged marriages still sometimes take place today in some Asian, Turkish, and Greek communities. In an arranged marriage, close family members select a girl to be bride, a boy to be groom. The selection process is based on financial considerations, perceived compatibility, friendship ties between the families, religion, and class or caste. For the marriage partners, it is assumed that love will follow marriage, rather than precede it.

The garlands used in this Hindu wedding ceremony symbolize the marriage bonds. In this religion, the marriage may have been arranged by the family, with the partners selected by the families. Arranged marriages can prove very successful.

In effect, many marriages in earlier centuries, in all countries, were arranged or at least encouraged by the families of the two partners. If the marriage was seen to be in trouble, the families would do everything that they could to save it. Separation was regarded as a possibility only after all serious attempts at reconciliation had failed.

Divorce in today's world

Talking point

"The genie of personal fulfillment won't go back in the bottle, but its volatility can be contained. In continental European countries with a Catholic tradition, terrifying grandmothers succeed in binding extended families together with a mixture of guilt and fear, even though there may be divorce or homosexuality or illegitimacy among the younger generations. There is continuity, even if it's the continuity of tyranny."

Francine Stock, journalist and broadcaster, speaking in 1993

Do you think you should limit your personal ambitions for the sake of your family?

The twentieth century, especially in Western countries, has witnessed sweeping changes in attitudes to divorce. Certainly social changes, such as longer life expectancy, greater independence for women, and the sexual revolution of the 1960s have all played their part; but it is difficult to assess the direct effect that these have had on the divorce rates of different countries.

Today, the United Kingdom divorce rate is the highest in the European Union, second only in the world to the United States and the former Soviet Union. In the last 90 years the United Kingdom has seen its divorce rate increase 1,000 times. One out of four children in the United Kingdom will experience their parents' divorce before the age of 16. Half of all children born in the United States will have to undergo this trauma. In England and Wales, divorce rates are highest for men between the ages of 30 and 34 and for women between the ages of 25 and 29. This age difference reflects the average ages at which men and women get married.

The United States has the highest divorce rate in the world. According to statistics, half of these North American teenagers will have experienced their parents' divorce.

Marital breakdown

It is clear that divorce rates have soared in the last 40 years. What is not clear, and is hard to evaluate, is whether or not the rates of marital breakdown have increased. "Marital breakdown" describes marriages that fail but end in separation, rather than divorce. It may be that the rates of marital breakdown are roughly the same as they were in previous decades, but that today people are much readier to end a marriage in divorce. Previously a couple may have separated or continued to live out an empty, unhappy marriage.

Divorce rate in the U.S., 1940 to present		
Year	Divorce rate among total population	Divorce rate among married women (15 and older)
1940	2.0%	8.8%
1946	4.3%	17.9%
1951	2.5%	9.9%
1957	2.2%	9.2%
1965	2.5%	10.6%
1970	3.5%	14.9%
1975	4.8%	20.3%
1979	5.3%	22.8%
1981	5.3%	22.6%
1985	5.0%	21.7%
1990	4.7%	20.9%
1993	4.6%	20.5%
1994	4.6%	20.5%

"No relationship should last longer than a fridge... and that's seven years."

The words of international model Twiggy during the 1960s

Today nearly 30 percent of divorces occur in marriages of five to nine years' duration; and, increasingly, it is the woman who sues for divorce. The most common ground on which a woman seeks divorce is "unreasonable behavior" by the husband. When a man seeks a divorce, the most common reason given is his wife's adultery. The likelihood of remarriage after divorce is now slightly lower than it was. Men are much more likely to remarry than women, and those who do usually do so within five years of their divorce.

25

Until recently in the United States, divorce laws required one marriage partner to petition for divorce by accusing the other of some kind of misconduct. This resulted in the "adversarial system," in which the partners, each represented by a lawyer, thrashed out a settlement. This confrontational process tended to be painful and damaging for the adults and for the children involved. The original concept of "fault" in divorce, which implied that one partner was specifically to blame, was amended from the 1940s onward. No-fault grounds began to be accepted, and the law came to recognize incompatibility or living apart as adequate grounds for divorce.

Children may become involved in their parents' disputes, which can cause them unbearable conflict of loyalties. They love both parents and cannot bear to see them hurting each other.

Marriage and divorce rates: European Union comparison, 1994 (rates per 1,000 population)

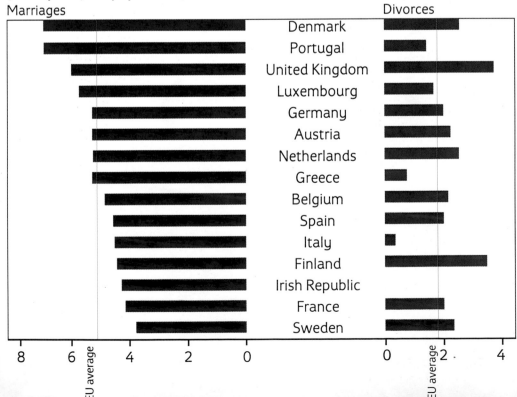

Marriages		Divorces
Denmark		
Portugal		
United Kingdom		
Luxembourg		
Germany		
Austria		
Netherlands		
Greece		
Belgium		
Spain		
Italy		
Finland		
Irish Republic		
France		
Sweden		

Marriages axis: 8 6 EU average 4 2 0

Divorces axis: 0 EU average 2 4

Do high divorce rates suggest that modern Western society condones divorce? Apparently not. Today, as in earlier times, the attitude that divorce signifies a moral failure increases feelings of guilt among divorcing couples. Along with guilt come feelings of regret: nearly one third of women and more than half of all men have feelings of nostalgia for their former spouse and claim to regret the collapse of their marriage. Many divorced couples feel that their legal advisors pushed them into a rapid settlement. The majority of experts—psychologists, sociologists, educators, and economists—are concerned about the breakdown of the institutions of marriage and family. They fear the effects on children of such widespread divorce, and they fear the cost to society in emotional, social, educational, and financial terms.

The Catholic Church

Within some cultures and religions, traditional attitudes to divorce remain central. In the Roman Catholic Church, a divorced couple is regarded "as still sacramentally married." Although the Catholic Church no longer forbids divorce, it does not formally recognize it either. The act of divorce is regarded as a civil matter. In the Catholic countries of Italy, Portugal, and Spain, divorce was illegal until the 1970s. Today, Spain and Italy have significantly lower divorce rates than other European countries.

"I divorced my first husband when I was twenty-four. We had absolutely nothing in common and I think I married him only in order to be seen to be properly grown up. [After the divorce] my father did not speak to me for over eight years. I met someone else, married him, and gave birth to our first child in those years. I used to visit [my parents'] house and have a cup of tea in the kitchen with my mother. My father would stay in the sitting room. It seems difficult to believe in this day and age that someone could disapprove so strongly of divorce.... But he did."

Forty-one-year-old English woman talking in 1990

The Muslim faith

According to Islamic law, a Muslim man can take up to four wives. The Koran states: "Marry as many women as you wish, two or three or four. If you fear not to treat them equally, marry only one. Indeed you will not be able to be just between your wives even if you try." This is usually taken to mean that it is preferable to have only one wife, as it would be difficult to treat four wives equally in terms of love and affection and in financial terms. When women were completely dependent on men in earlier centuries and it was almost impossible to manage alone, it probably made sense for a man to marry as many as he could afford. Today, Muslim men need to be wealthy to afford more than one wife, and many Muslim women are less likely to tolerate such an arrangement.

Divorce rates in Muslim countries and among followers of the Muslim faith are significantly lower than those of the West.

Divorce "without lawful necessity" is frowned upon in Islam, and all possible attempts are made to reconcile couples who are considering divorce. Before their divorce becomes final, a couple must live together for a three-month period known as 'iddah, during which time they are expected to work out their problems. The husband must continue to support the wife financially during this period. Having said that, it is much simpler for a man than a woman to obtain a divorce. He simply goes to a marriage registrar and, before witnesses, announces that the marriage is ended. If his wife wishes to attend, they can go as a couple. But if a wife wants to end her marriage, she has to take the case to court and prove beyond all doubt that her husband has broken his marriage contract.

International comparison of divorce rates (per 1,000 population)		
Japan	1995	1.6%
U.S.	1993	4.6%
Germany	1993	1.9%
France	1991	1.9%
Italy	1993	0.4%
U.K.	1992	3.0%
Sweden	1993	2.5%

"I have been divorced three times.... I was very young when I first married. I was in Holland, she was Dutch, I barely spoke the language. As I became more fluent and I got to know her better, I started to wonder what on earth I had done. I hadn't had a girlfriend before—you don't in the Muslim culture. You don't even go out unaccompanied with a single woman. Marriages are normally made through introductions by one of the family members. The marriage simply petered out. My second marriage was much stronger and I think it could have succeeded. My second wife was given to jealousy, which didn't help the relationship, and we were both working hard. We did have a lot of fights about housework and about money—but I did not see that as a reason to end the marriage. It was she who wanted the divorce. I honestly think that the only reason I married my third wife was that I was lonely— and I was drinking fairly heavily. Most of my friends and family could see that it was a mistake from the outset... but you don't see things like that for yourself when you think you are in love. I don't feel any desire to marry again. What would be the point?"

Fifty-six-year-old Turkish Muslim man talking in 1996

Case study

Sarah and Yiannis married soon after they met on the island of Crete at the beginning of the 1980s. But their marriage could not withstand the pressures that their different backgrounds brought to bear upon it....

Sarah had gone to Crete on vacation with a girlfriend. Yiannis attached himself to them, and soon he and Sarah became inseparable. Within a year, Sarah was pregnant with their first child. It was then that the problems started. Sarah wanted to return to London for the birth of the baby, but Yiannis and his mother believed that the baby should be born on Crete. So began a continuing struggle between Sarah and her mother-in-law, who wanted to have a say in every household decision. While parental intervention was more or less accepted in Greek culture, Sarah came from a different culture and found her mother-in-law's attitude difficult to tolerate.

Sarah's two children both had to accept that if they lived in their mother's home country, they would have to leave their father in his home country. They see their father only on his occasional visits.

While the baby was young, Sarah and Yiannis lived in London. But Yiannis was very close to his family and became homesick, so they moved back to Crete. There his mother was in charge to such an extent that she decided when the water would be switched on and off, when the family would eat, and who it was acceptable for Sarah to be friendly with and who not. Sarah was not even allowed to drive, for fear she would have an accident. She was expected to defer to her husband's every wish and behave like a proper Greek wife. This way of life became increasingly miserable for Sarah, who had had her own job, house, and car in London for years before she met Yiannis.

When Sarah became pregnant again, she decided to return home. She wanted both her children to be educated in England, and she had become increasingly disillusioned and unhappy with her Greek life. But her husband opposed the idea of her return to England and without his permission she could not raise sufficient money to make the journey. She found herself, effectively, a prisoner. When Sarah investigated the possibility of divorce, she found that there was a real danger of losing her children if she elected to return to London. The children, it seemed, would stay on Crete.

Looking back, it seems that some of the problems Sarah and Yiannis encountered could have been resolved with mediation and with more understanding on both sides. As it is, Sarah has succeeded, with considerable difficulty, in moving herself and the two children to London but has been unable to get a divorce. Yiannis visits for three months every year.

Yiannis has lost day-to-day contact with his children as a result of the collapse of his marriage. He misses them greatly but cannot see a way out of the dilemma caused by the separation.

The legal issues

Talking point

"Children are much more likely to avoid the harmful effects of divorce if they live with the parent of the same sex [as themselves]. There is no reason to believe that mothers have the monopoly on competence at bringing up children. Fathers can do just as well, and in some cases better."

Richard A. Warshak, professor of psychology and author of *The Custody Revolution*

Who do you think fare best at bringing up children—mothers or fathers?

The legal process of divorce includes the issue of whom the children are to live with (residence) and the division of the family's finances and assets (property). If the couple can resolve these matters through discussion between themselves, the financial cost of divorce can be greatly reduced. Once lawyers, and possibly the courts, become involved, there are additional costs and less money is left for the family. Most couples find that they run into difficulties or cannot agree, so they each employ a lawyer to act on their behalf. Lengthy and bitter legal battles between divorcing couples can scar both parents and children.

Mediation services, in which an objective third party helps the marriage partners sort out their practical problems, can vastly reduce the financial cost of divorce.

In many Western countries today, efforts are being made to help couples who are thinking about divorce. In England, Wales, and Northern Ireland, the Family Law Act of 1996 states that couples must attend an information-giving session, which tells them about the likely consequences of divorce and makes them aware of the roles of mediation and counseling services. If a couple expresses a desire for counseling and if there is a chance that a marriage can be saved, they may be referred to a marriage counselor who will help them work together on understanding, improving, and preserving their relationship. Even if the marriage does not survive, access to divorce counseling can give a greater understanding and insight into the events that have led to the decision to divorce.

Reducing conflict

Mediation services provide an opportunity for couples to sit down together with an impartial third party (the mediator) and look at ways to sort out practical problems like money, accommodation, and contact with the children. Mediation is intended to cut down the amount of time and money spent in legal negotiations, in which each parent instructs a lawyer. It is known that mediation and counseling reduce conflict between couples.

Financial matters that a couple needs to consider may include the division of property (a house or apartment), joint possessions, car(s), life insurance policies, shares, and pensions. How these assets are divided reflects the earning power of each parent. The past, present, and future working opportunities of both parents are taken into account. As men tend to earn more than women, it is usually the husband who is required to pay support for the children and perhaps for his ex-wife as well, although in some cases it is the wife who supports the husband. Maintenance payments for a nonworking parent who has care of the children are considered, but are not granted automatically. The major earner usually pays maintenance for the children until their education is complete, as well as private school fees if applicable. The cost of child care, when both parents are working, is also taken into account.

In some countries, such as the United States, couples may organize settlements before they marry. These legal agreements make financial and practical provision in advance for each partner in the event of divorce.

What if one partner declines to divorce?

If one spouse is reluctant or refuses to divorce, a divorce can usually be granted by the courts after five years, provided that the couple have lived apart during these years, on the grounds that the marriage has irretrievably broken down.

Which parent should the child live with?

Traditionally it has been accepted that, in cases of divorce, the children should stay with the mother. This reflects the fact that women are usually more actively involved with taking care of their children than men are.

Until recently, the law has tended to grant custody and care of children to the mother, on the basis that she is the most appropriate person to look after them (unless the courts find her unfit to do so). In the West, the majority of children of divorcing parents stay with their mother, and the father is usually granted the right to visit his children at regular intervals. In recent years, however, an increasing number of fathers are being granted custody of their children. In the United States and

Europe, about 15 percent of children of divorced parents live with their fathers. Joint care and control of the children has also become more common, with parents sharing responsibility for their upbringing.

Some experts believe that children, especially boys, may thrive in the custody of their father rather than with their mother.

However, research suggests that children in France are increasingly likely to be brought up by their fathers. In 1993, legislation in France made joint care and control of children obligatory; in other words, all major decisions concerning the child had to be agreed upon by both parents. Joint care and control is the exception rather than the rule in the United States. Some of the most bitter battles seen in the divorce courts in the United States have resulted from the practice of granting custody to one parent or the other, rather than to both.

When a Muslim couple divorces, any children under the age of seven tend to live with their mother, but boys over the age of seven are expected to live with their fathers. However, in exceptional circumstances it may be considered in the child's best interests to live with the father in infancy.

One of the important issues that emerges during divorce negotiations is that, while husband and wife may divorce each other, the couple remain parents to their children for life.

Janine and her husband ended up in a legal battle over their divorce.

Case study

Janine, a thirty-one-year-old British woman, talks about the problems she and her ex-husband encountered over the legal aspects of their divorce.

"We were together for nearly ten years. It was always a very passionate, turbulent, sometimes violent relationship. But it was heady, exciting, and never dull. In the end we came to the point where we realized that we could lead more harmonious, easier, more gentle lives with other partners. We decided to split up. We sat down one evening and made a list of everything in the house and agreed, between us, who was to have what. We decided on the financial split and on who was to keep the house. It was almost a blueprint for an amicable divorce.

"As agreed, I saw a lawyer and asked him to act for us. That was the first problem. He advised me that my husband should be represented by another lawyer, not himself. My husband then retained a lawyer—and that's when the problems started. From then on things acquired a momentum of their own. The process, by definition, became adversarial.

"Each lawyer presented the other with long lists of questions and long tracts of justifications for the questions. It was all, I understand, so that both could be seen to be doing their legal duty by each of us. Unfortunately, it had the effect of souring my relationship with my husband that, up until then, had been sensible and cooperative. Every single last thing became an issue. Even the value of our respective cars was questioned in an attempt by both lawyers to divide everything equitably. But, the point is, we had already decided for ourselves what we wanted. We didn't want a couple of strangers delving into every corner of our lives. It led to many rows. Each of us blamed the other— we could not see at that time that it was the lawyers who were upping the ante. We both genuinely wanted an amicable divorce for the sake of the children. But things simply got out of our control."

The effects of divorce on children

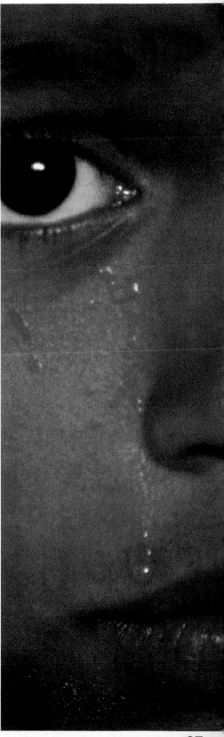

Talking point

"As children of the sixties, we all thought we could do exactly as we liked... we were free. We never gave a thought to our children. We simply thought that if we were happy, they would be happy. People believed at that time better a good divorce than a bad marriage."

Fifty-two-year-old American woman

"Children have to live within the world created for them by others. The quality of their future lives as parents and partners depends on the provision of a positive rather than a negative blueprint of family life to carry with them into adulthood."

Monica Cockett and John Tripp in their introduction to
Caught in the Middle, 1997

These quotations illustrate contrasting views about adult responsibility toward children. Do you agree with either—or both—of them?

For adults, divorce—although painful—is often the best solution to an unhappy or abusive marriage. And until relatively recently many experts (including psychiatrists, psychologists, sociologists, and lawyers) considered that a child would be happier and more emotionally stable living with one contented parent than with two unhappy parents. In the 1960s and 1970s this accepted way of thinking led to the relaxation of the divorce laws in many Western countries. No one could be sure that easier divorce laws would bring greater happiness: it was simply assumed to be the case.

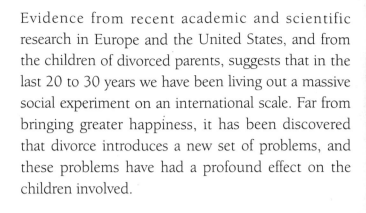

Evidence from recent academic and scientific research in Europe and the United States, and from the children of divorced parents, suggests that in the last 20 to 30 years we have been living out a massive social experiment on an international scale. Far from bringing greater happiness, it has been discovered that divorce introduces a new set of problems, and these problems have had a profound effect on the children involved.

Girls from stepfamilies are far more likely to become single teenage mothers than girls from intact families.

The effects can be severe and may last for many years. They may affect a child's employment prospects and his or her potential as a marriage partner and parent. This is not to say that all children of divorced parents suffer such severe and long-lasting effects. Some do, while others do to a lesser extent and for a shorter time. Experts say that the crisis period after divorce lasts about two years. In other words, it takes about two years for a child to accept her or his new life.

A pattern for divorce

The effects of divorce on children are underlined by the following United Kingdom statistics. Children of stepfamilies are three times more likely to leave home before the age of 18 than the children of intact families. They are more likely to leave school at the minimum age and less likely to go to college. Girls from stepfamilies are twice as likely to become single teenage mothers and three times more likely to marry before the age of 20 (early marriage itself being a contributory factor to the divorce rate).

The emotional effects

On learning that their parents are to divorce, children may experience shock, anger, anxiety, uncertainty, loneliness, guilt, shame, and profound misery. They may become either aggressive or withdrawn. Very few children want their parents to split up, even though the family atmosphere may be unhappy and turbulent. But the emotional effects on children may be greater if the parents fail to explain the situation to them. It is important that children are told what is happening and what will happen to them in the future. The way children are told, and how much they are told, should be tailored to their age. Having said that, researchers have found that even in cases where children have been given full and careful explanations, the children later claim not to have been told very much or not to have been told anything at all.

Girls of divorced parents may become verbally aggressive. Boys in this situation may get into trouble outside the home.

Sometimes the immediate effects on children may be gauged by what they say and how they behave. But some children may say very little, barely listening to what their parents say and putting as much space between themselves and the family home as possible. In this way they erect a protective barrier around themselves. Sometimes children do not believe that their parents are splitting up and hope that they will get back together again. Some children continue to wish for this even after one or the other, or both, of their parents has re-married a new partner.

"She had a total nervous breakdown. I didn't see it coming because you don't think of children having nervous breakdowns. She became incontinent, she didn't move, she was totally traumatized."

Divorced mother of a two-and-a-half-year-old girl, speaking on BBC-TV, 1994

Children of divorced parents often experience conflicting emotions. It is difficult for children to accept that their parents no longer love each other but that they will continue to love and care for their child.

Children have great difficulty in accepting that the departing parent still loves them—otherwise, why are they leaving? Young children place absolute faith in their parents' judgments and suffer unbearable inner conflicts when their parents find it actually impossible to live together under the same roof. It is painful and confusing for a child to be told, on the one hand, that one of her parents is going to leave and, on the other, that this parent loves her just the same.

The social effects

Children whose parents have divorced become less confident in their social relationships and friendships. They begin to fear that if one parent can leave them then so can the other. Their sense of general well-being can be profoundly undermined. Many children feel powerless to alter the course of events of the divorce process, and, as a result, they may become aggressive or difficult. Young children may regress and start bed-wetting again.

Some children undergoing their parents' separation and divorce become silent, withdrawn, and moody and find it increasingly difficult to get along with school friends.

Children may find that their own friendships are threatened. This can happen because their friends are still living within an intact family. Children living through divorce will naturally be drawn to other children in the same position as themselves. They may become more dependent in their friendships or find it difficult to make friends as a consequence of their own depression and loss of self-

confidence. If the divorce prompts a change of school or a move to a new area, children are faced with a further set of difficulties and are required to form new friendships at a time at which it may be difficult for them to do so.

Children of divorcing parents may become increasingly depressed and unable to concentrate on their schoolwork and homework.

The educational effects

Children living through divorce may find their lives becoming increasingly chaotic. They may be late to bed and late to school and pay less attention to homework. They will find that their parents probably have less time and energy to make sure that homework is being done properly. Children may be unwilling to go to school and, when they do go, may find it difficult to concentrate and fully participate in lessons. As a consequence of the stress in their lives, they may become ill or they may develop psychosomatic illnesses (typically, headaches, stomachaches, and nausea), which keep them away from school.

The financial effects

With divorce, two households must be created from one. So now there are two mortgage or rent bills, two electricity bills, two telephone bills, two household tax bills, two gas bills, two water bills, where before there was only one of each. This inevitably proves more expensive for the two parents and there is less disposable cash for vacations, toys, clothes, shoes, and pocket money. Divorce almost certainly means, for everyone, that the family's disposable income will be quite considerably reduced.

In their adult lives, children of divorced parents continue to be penalized. Research now shows that the career prospects and earning potential for children of divorced parents are less promising than for children of intact families.

Many children feel isolated during parental divorce. They may mourn the absence of their departed parent for up to two years. Some may take up to five years fully to accept their new situation.

"Although most children do not exhibit acute difficulties beyond the stage of family breakdown, a significant minority of children encounter long-term problems."

The Exeter Family Study, 1994

Case study

Gary's parents divorced when he was 13, eight years ago. Gary has not seen his father since he was 14.

"He used to come and see me on weekends sometimes. He took me to a soccer game once, which was great. But then he stopped coming. My Mom was really upset about the divorce. She kept saying he was a real bastard, which I hated. I didn't want to hear that. Dad used to help me with some of my homework, but after he went there was no

one to help. In fact, I couldn't really be bothered doing it any more. I couldn't see the point. Who was to know anyway?

"I started skipping school, just for a laugh with a couple of other boys. We used to hang around the stores, try stuff on, you know, just mess around. We started stealing things.... It was so easy. Just take it and run. No one tried to stop us. We started getting more and more stuff and selling it cheap to other boys at school. We started going to other towns, because we were afraid we might be recognized. We were taking stuff out in armfuls. There was nothing they could do—because we could run faster than any of them. Right then my Mom was in a terrible state. No way did she have any idea of what I was doing during the day.

As a teenage child of divorcing parents, Gary began to play hooky from school and became involved in petty crime.

"Well, one day the inevitable happened. We got caught with a good haul of stuff—CDs. And then everything came out. The police found stuff in my room and in some of my friends' houses. They checked with the school and found out that I hadn't been near it for weeks. The school found out that I had been throwing away letters they had written to my Mom. Mom went absolutely ballistic: 'How could you do this to me?' and all that.

"Well, I was grounded then all right. I had to go to school, had to do my homework, had to face reality. I had to accept that my Dad wasn't coming back. I had to grow up fast. My criminal record has made a difference about what sort of jobs I can apply for.... Obviously I can't go in for anything where money or security is involved. I can't say what life holds for me now—just have to see, I guess."

How children feel about divorce

Talking point

"My husband is Algerian—and Muslim—so when we split up I lost my son. In the Muslim culture, boys over the age of seven must live with their father—and that's all there is to it. It would have been pointless to try and do anything about it. I know that my son at that age wanted to stay with me... but there was no choice in the matter."

A thirty-three-year-old Dutch woman talking in 1996

Do you think that children of divorced parents should have more say about whom they live with, whatever culture they belong to?

The degree of responsibility shouldered by children during the time of their parents' divorce, and afterward, can be tremendous. An older child will be encouraged to help more with the younger ones. The older child may also become best friend and confidant to the resident parent. Sometimes parents, in their own anguish and regret over their divorce, overlook the feelings of their children.

Many children feel guilty and blame themselves for their parents' separation. Some promise to be "good" if the departing parent comes back. It is very difficult for young children to realize that adults have a relationship between themselves that is independent of their relationship with their children. After the divorce, contact with the absent parent is essential for the child's well-being and healthy development. Sadly, nearly half of all parents who do not have custody (usually the father) lose all contact with their children within two years of the divorce. Research suggests that many fathers who lose contact with their families feel that it is better for the children, because the contact itself can be too distressing.

Many children find it difficult to accept their new lives when they may be seeing their father only on weekends. They may need time to adjust to being with Dad rather than with Mom. Very young children do better if the times away from the parent who has custody are kept short at first.

When parents remarry

Divorce, for a child, is a long process. It starts with the breakdown of the parents' marriage and continues through the difficulties of separation and divorce to a different life, usually with one or the other parent, after the divorce. At some stage one or both parents may decide to marry a second time.

47

Remarriage, and the introduction of stepparents and possibly stepbrothers and stepsisters, presents the child with new problems. The parent and the new partner, naturally, want the child or children to be as happy as they are. However, for many children, the knowledge that their parent is to remarry often only serves as a bleak confirmation that their natural parents will never again live together.

Children may feel threatened or positively jealous of their stepfamily. They may believe that their parent now has less time for them—which may indeed be the case if the parent is preoccupied with his or her new partner. They may find it difficult to accept the stepparent in any role of authority, and conflicts may arise that threaten the harmony of the new family.

"We were always fighting, always, that's what we liked doing. Mom and Dad were always at us to stop it, they would send us to our rooms, they would stop our allowance, they would say that we couldn't go out to play. Mom said once if you don't stop it, I'll leave and never come back. And she did. I felt as if I had actually killed her."

A fourteen-year-old boy talking about his parents' separation

Many children today have to learn to accept a new partner living with one or both of their parents. Initially they may not like them, seeing them as a threat or as an indication that things will never be the same again.

Case study

Emily's mother and father divorced when she was 11. She remembers it vividly:

"I felt as if my world had literally crashed into pieces. Dad told us that he was not going to live with us anymore. He said that we would see him on weekends, not every weekend, but alternate ones. I didn't know what he meant at first. I just didn't understand. I asked him if he would be there the next evening... and he just said "No." Mom was crying and crying. I felt sick. I started to try and do my homework because it had to be handed in the next day... but all I could think of was my Dad and where he was going. I couldn't do my homework. Mom said she would write me a note to take to school to say why I didn't do it. But I didn't want her telling everybody. I went to bed and couldn't sleep. I went into Mom's bed and then I did sleep, but later I woke up with a nightmare. Mom said everything was all right, so I thought Dad had come back. But he hadn't.

Emily has found it extremely difficult to accept her parents' divorce. She has needed a lot of support from her family and friends.

"When I woke up that first morning, I thought, no, it's not true. Dad's coming back. I felt sick again. I didn't go to school that day. My grandmother came and she was talking a long time to Mom. I don't know what they were talking about. Mom was crying nearly all day. She forgot to feed our cat.

"There was a program on TV that night, usually I watched it with Dad... but he wasn't there. Mom didn't want to watch it. She was on the telephone for ages. I miss my Dad like anything. Why can't he stay here with us?"

The effects of divorce on society

Professional counselors can often help children with the emotional strain and conflicts of loyalty they may experience while undergoing parental divorce. The content of the meetings between child and counselor remains confidential.

The principal effects of divorce on society are economic and social. Research by social scientists has shown that the effects may be serious, wide-ranging, and long lasting. Some of the economic effects include the need for more housing, as households split from one into two; more money for social services and benefit funds as more single women with children become dependent on the state welfare system; more money for the state health system as increasing numbers of people succumb to stress-related illnesses; more money to pay a greater number of trained counselors to help children and adults cope psychologically with the

Talking point

Expenditure on legal aid in matrimonial and family proceedings has risen two and a half times between 1989–1990 and 1993–1994.

Source: Legal Aid Board findings, UK, 1994

If people wish to divorce, but cannot afford the legal fees, do you think the state should help them financially?

process of divorce; and more funds for legal aid so that people on low incomes can secure legal advice and representation for their divorce proceedings.

It is generally true to say that the social effects of divorce cost society money either directly or indirectly. The social effects may include the following: an increasing number of children being brought up with only one parent; increased rates of illness and stress in association with the rising divorce rate (for children, many experts believe that the loss of a parent through divorce causes even greater stress than bereavement); an increase in teenage pregnancies; the weakening of the institution of marriage, which is regarded by many as a secure and stable framework in which to bring up children; and an increase in delinquency rates. However, some studies suggest that delinquency in children is less the result of divorce than of problems with their home life. If there is a lack of support for children at home, it may make little difference whether or not the parents remain together.

People going through divorce are often under very considerable stress and may find it helpful to discuss some of their problems with their family doctor.

Despite the high divorce rate in many countries, the motherless or fatherless family is less common today than it was a hundred years ago. Although few families in the nineteenth century were broken by divorce, many were broken by death. Some recent research into stepparent families has indicated that the children are as happy, productive, and successful as children in intact families. Other research, however, indicates that social problems increase through the generations. As teenagers, children of divorced parents are likely to claim either that they will never marry or that when they marry they will do so for life. Statistically, however, they are more likely to end their marriages in divorce.

Is marriage under threat?

Some people believe that, with a decreasing marriage rate and an increasing divorce rate, the system of marriage will eventually collapse. This does not appear to be the case, given the high number of remarriages. But remarriages are more vulnerable than first marriages; twice as many remarriages as first marriages end in divorce. In spite of this, marriage and family life continue to be profoundly important in most cultures and religions. The statistics don't seem to put people off.

> "Following divorce there is a growing social and legal expectation that couples will maintain a civil (meaning both 'civilized' and 'legal') relationship until the children reach a minimum age of 18. This socially and legally mandated continuity asks a lot of people who could not tolerate living together."
>
> From *Marital Breakdown and the Health of the Nation*, One Plus One, London, 1995

The institution of marriage has seen numerous changes in the last hundred years. Many women now work on a full-time or part-time basis, usually combining work with looking after children. A husband may still be the main breadwinner, but some husbands take on the bulk of child care duties or share them with their wives.

The future

The harmful effects upon children of parental separation and divorce may be kept to a minimum if they have the love and support of their families and friends.

Research now shows that the process of separation and divorce can be harmful to children in many different areas of their lives. In the future how should society tackle the subject of divorce? Far from turning the clock back to an era in which divorce was difficult to obtain, current thinking in the West suggests that divorce should be made a less painful process for all concerned. What society must do, however, is attach a greater importance to the effects of divorce on children.

Couples can give greater thought to the processes of mediation and professional counseling, aimed at reducing hostility and anger between divorcing parents. The benefits of mediation and conciliation, proven by research, are now completely accepted by many Western governments. Children should be helped to survive the processes of separation and divorce in order to minimize any serious, long-lasting effects; they need support from their families and from friends, continuing contact with the parent who leaves the family home, and the opportunity for professional counseling if appropriate. When divorce is inevitable, it is important that both the adults and the children concerned see it as a positive step, as the way forward out of a painful situation into a new and, it is to be hoped, happier one.

Stable and happy marriages

The best way to avoid the pain of divorce is to make a stable and successful marriage. And the best way to create more stable marriages is for all of us to give serious thought to the choice of a life partner and co-parent. "Marry in haste, repent at leisure," as the saying goes. There is no need to make a hasty teenage marriage in the social climate of today's Western world. To make a lasting and happy marriage it is vital to acquire the skills necessary to keep a relationship strong. The ability to communicate effectively and to manage situations of conflict in a positive way is most important.

A 1990 survey of thirteen European countries listed the following factors for a successful marriage in order of importance.

	France	Great Britain	W.Germany	Italy	Spain	Portugal	Netherlands	Belgium	N.Ireland	Ireland	Denmark	Sweden	Norway	Average of 13 nations
Mutual respect and appreciation	84	84	79	90	80	83	92	86	83	83	83	91	93	85.5
Faithfulness	74	90	78	84	81	77	88	85	94	93	81	89	90	84.9
Understanding and tolerance	73	86	77	79	74	75	85	77	81	81	80	88	84	80.0
Happy sexual relationship	67	66	50	67	63	68	62	64	69	67	65	66	62	64.3
Children	64	57	44	64	72	65	54	54	69	62	42	61	60	59.1
Living apart from your in-laws	62	53	37	46	33	53	60	56	54	46	53	53	41	49.8
Tastes and interests in common	38	49	48	49	43	51	29	39	39	40	20	30	23	38.3
An adequate income	38	34	26	32	40	48	27	45	40	52	10	22	21	33.5
Good housing	36	37	25	25	34	52	36	39	36	46	30	40	23	35.3
Sharing household chores	35	44	21	30	33	49	34	38	45	38	48	48	33	38.2
Shared religious beliefs	16	19	14	26	28	34	19	22	37	33	16	18	24	23.5
Same social background	21	20	12	17	24	25	23	22	21	25	11	12	14	19.0
Agreement on politics	7	7	7	10	10	15	8	9	10	4	4	10	7	8.0

Recognition of problems

What steps should couples take to limit the damage if their marriage is in trouble? First, they need to accept that they have problems and be prepared to talk to each other about them. If that does not help, then they need to talk to someone else. The worst thing a couple can do is to keep the problem to themselves. For those people who do not wish to talk to family or close friends about their marriage problems, the best option is to seek help through the family doctor, who will be able to put them in touch with a suitable professional counselor. If marital stress and discord are recognized early and dealt with through counseling, a marriage may well stand a better chance of surviving. Schools, workplaces, and social workers can also do their part in disseminating information about how to make a healthy, happy marriage and how to seek effective counseling and practical help should the marriage come under intolerable strains.

Once problems in the family have been recognized, professionally trained counselors can provide family or marital therapy. Members of the family may attend sessions together or, if they prefer, alone.

The alternatives to divorce

• reconciliation (perhaps through marriage counseling or with the help of family and friends)
• trial separation (in which each partner has a breathing space to think clearly about the situation)
• legal separation (without divorce)
• a marriage in which both partners lead completely separate lives
• an open marriage in which both partners agree that they may take a lover as and when they feel like it
• polygamy (taking more than one wife, as has been the custom in some Muslim countries and in the Mormon religion) or bigamy (taking a second wife when still married to the first—illegal in most countries)

The marriage of Prince Charles and Lady Diana Spencer in 1982 ended in divorce. It is possible that the marriage could have worked if both partners had been willing to recognize and discuss their marital problems at an early stage.

As developing countries make technological advances and move toward greater industrialization, it will be interesting to see whether or not they follow the patterns of divorce seen in the West. Or will traditional attitudes persist, with family and friends continuing to be involved in making marriages and keeping them together? A systematic program of relationship education concerned with marital breakdown could help people in these countries avoid making some of the mistakes we have made in the West.

The greatest hope for reducing the divorce rate in the West is a broad-ranging educational program combined with a widespread availability of professional counseling services. Many marriages could be saved if couples went to counseling rather than to the lawyer's office. Now that we know so much more about divorce—the emotional pain, the long-term psychological disadvantages, the economic costs, and the costs to society—we all owe it to ourselves to do the best we can to keep our marriages strong and to put high values on the interests of our children.

"We give each other freedom to pursue our own interests and to see our own friends. We try not to be possessive of one another. We do not involve the children in any arguments or differences that we may have."

Dutch man talking in 1997 about his successful 25-year marriage

Despite high divorce rates in the West, the majority of marriages survive.

Case study

Lydia and Susannah's parents divorced when Lydia was eight and Susannah was six. Lydia, now age 30, tells their story:

"Our parents had very little in common. They married when they were very young—our mother was only 20. My father had a lot of outside interests—politics and other things—which my mother found pretty dull. She was lonely and bored and she thought she would be happier without him. I can understand all that now, but of course I didn't when I was eight.

After her parents divorced, Lydia saw her father every two weeks. She now appreciates the value of these visits.

"They divorced and my father went to live in Delft, which was more than one hour away by train. We had to go and see him every other weekend. I just hated those journeys. I really hated them. I didn't really speak to my father for nearly two years. I just endured the visits. I hated the upheaval. I liked my own room in my own home. I didn't want to go away every other weekend. I felt like a gypsy.

"I had no idea of the value of the visits or what they were intended for. I do wish that someone had been able to explain to us in terms we could understand that this regular contact would prove very valuable and beneficial to us in our adult lives. I think it would all have been easier to accept had I seen that there was a point to it.

"I'm happy to say that now my father is really close to me and to my sister, and I certainly love him. I can see the value of those weekend visits now— how otherwise would we have really known him? He used to take us to see his parents, our grandparents, and we would not otherwise have kept in contact with them. I think he really did his best to minimize the trauma of it all for us... and of course he desperately wanted to see us. He didn't even really want the divorce, although I do think in the end he was happy with it."

Glossary

Adversarial system A system that encourages conflict. In legal cases there are two opponents—a plaintiff and a defendant—each of whom is seeking to prove that he or she is right and the opponent is wrong. This is known as the adversarial system.

Adversary Enemy, opponent.

Bereavement The loss of a relative or friend, usually by death; although the word is also used to describe the end of a relationship by divorce or separation.

Caste A system of social classes. Usually applied to the social divisions found in India.

Counseling A process by which a professional person assists someone with social, personal, or emotional problems.

Delinquency A type of behavior resulting in minor crime. Usually applied to young people as "juvenile delinquency."

Divorce petition A formal written request to the court for the legal dissolution (end) of a marriage.

Extended family A family in which grandparents, aunts, uncles, and cousins live in the same area (sometimes in the same home) and share family responsibilities.

Fault Guilt, offense, responsibility for wrongdoing. The "fault" system of divorce involves one marriage partner proving that the other partner is to blame, or at fault.

Grounds (for divorce) Basis, motive, or reason for divorce.

Maintenance A husband's or wife's provision, in the form of money, for their former marriage partner after separation or divorce. Maintenance enables the custodial partner and the children of the marriage to be fed, clothed, and housed.

Marriage registrar An official who keeps the register of marriage. The registrar's office is an office in which civil marriages are conducted and in which births, marriages, and deaths are recorded with the issue of certificates.

Mediation A process by which an independent third party helps to resolve the financial and practical differences of divorcing or separating couples with a minimum of anger and argument.

No-fault divorce A divorce that is based on the grounds that the partners no longer wish to live together or remain married. It is accepted that two people can decide to divorce without having to state grounds, or reasons, for their decision. In the past divorce could only be granted on certain grounds, such as, for example, adultery or desertion.

Protestant Reformation The sixteenth-century movement that reformed the principles and practices of the Roman Catholic Church. It is believed to have started in 1517 when Martin Luther issued 95 documents criticizing some of the principles and corrupt practices of the Roman Catholic Church. The Reformation of the Roman Catholic Church ended with the formation of the Protestant Church. Followers of the new church became known as Protestants after the declaration (*protestatio*) of Luther and his supporters. All Protestants rejected the authority of the pope, and sought guidance instead in the text of the Scriptures. Broadly, Protestant Churches include all Christian Churches except for Catholic and Eastern churches.

Reconcile To settle a dispute and restore harmony.

Reconciliation A reuniting of friends, family, or marriage partners.

Spouse Husband or wife.

Intact family The current term for a family that has retained its original structure or order: the children of the marriage live with both their natural parents. There are no stepsisters or stepbrothers and no half sisters or half brothers.

Judicial separation The separation of a wife and husband by the decision of a court—essentially a legal separation. Separation does not necessarily mean divorce.

Stepfamily A family that is connected by law rather than by blood. A child's stepfather is his or her mother's new husband. A child's stepmother is his or her father's new wife. A child's stepsister is the daughter of a step-parent from that stepparent's former marriage. A child's stepbrother is the son of a stepparent from that step-parent's former marriage. Stepfamilies can include stepgrandparents, step-cousins, stepaunts, and stepuncles.

Books to Read

For Younger Readers

Berry, Joy. *About Divorce*. Danbury, CT: Children's Press, 1994.

Bolick, Nancy O'Keefe. *How to Survive Your Parents' Divorce*. Danbury, CT: Franklin Watts, 1995.

Blume, Judy. *It's Not the End of the World*. New York: A Yearling Book, 1986.

Fine, Anne B. *Step by Wicked Step*. Boston: Little Brown, 1996.

Ford, Melanie, et al. *My Parents Are Divorced, Too: A Book for Kids by Kids*.Pasadena, CA: Magination Press, 1997.

Goldentyer, Debra. *Parental Divorce* (Teen Hot Line). Austin, TX: Raintree Steck-Vaughn,. 1995.

Harrison, Michael. *It's My Life*. New York: Holiday House, 1998.

Rosenberg, Maxine B. *Living With a Single Parent*. New York: Simon & Schuster Children's Books, 1992.

Sachs, Marilyn. *Another Day*. New York: Dutton Children's Books, 1997.

Schneider, Meg. *Difficult Questions Kids Ask and Are Too Afraid to Ask About Divorce*. New York: Fireside Books, 1996.

For Older and Adult Readers

Ahrons, Constance R. and Roy H. Rodgers. *Divorced Families: Meeting the Challenge of Divorce and Remarriage*. New York: W. W. Norton Co., 1989.

Difonzo, J. Herbie. *Beneath the Fault Line: The Popular.and Legal Culture of Divorce in Twentieth-Century America*. University Press of Virginia, 1997.

Furstenberg, Frank F. and Andrew J. Cherlin. *Divided Families: What Happens to Children When Parents Part*. Cambridge, MA: Harvard University Press, 1994.

Gallagher, Maggie. *The Abolition of Marriage: How We Destroy Lasting Love*. Washington, D.C.: Regnery Publishers, 1996.

Garden, Jenny. *The (Almost) Painless Divorce: What Your Lawyer Won't Tell You*. Louisville, KY: Evanston Publishers, 1996.

Garrity, Carla B. and Mitchell A. Baris. *Caught in the Middle: Protecting the Children of High-Conflict Divorce*. Jossey Bass Books, 1997.

Jowell, Barbara Tom. *After He's Gone: A Guide for Widowed and Divorced Women*. Birch Lane Press, 1997.

Krantzler, Mel. *Divorcing*. New York: St. Martin's Press, 1992.

Ostman, Ellen D. *Dear Client: Complete Handbook for Understanding and Surviving Your Legal Divorce Process*. Tampa, FL: Axelrod Publishing of Tampa Bay, 1996.

Splinter, John P. *Complete Divorce Recovery Handbook* (Lifelines for Recovery). New York: HarperCollins , 1992.

Trafford, Abigail. *Crazy Time: Surviving Divorce and Building a New Life*. New York: Harper Perennial, 1993.

Useful Addresses

Academy of Family Mediators
4 Militia Drive
Lexington, MA 02173
Telephone: (617) 674-2663

American Association for Counseling and
International Association of Counseling
Services Inc.,
5999 Stevenson Avenue
Alexandria, VA 22304
Telephone: (703) 823-9800

Association of Family and Conciliation Courts
(AFCC)
329 West Wilson Street
Madison, WI 53703
Telephone: (608) 251-4001

Divorce Lifeline
6920 Two Twentieth Street South West
Suite K
Mountlake Terrace, Washington 98043
Telephone: (206) 461-3222

Parents Without Partners
7910 Woodmont Avenue
Washington, DC 20014
Telephone: (202) 638-1320

Further Information
Hot Lines

The Nineline
1-800-999-9999

Youth Crisis Hotline
1-800-448-4663

National Runaway Switchboard
1-800-621-4000

Community Information and Referral Services
1-800-352-3792

Website
Divorce Home Page
http://www.divorcesupport.com/index.html

Index

Numbers in **bold** refer to illustrations.